Oxford Progressive English R
General Editor: D.H. Ho

Stories of Shakespeare's Plays 1

The *Oxford Progressive English Readers* series provides a wide range of reading for learners of English. It includes classics, the favourite stories of young readers, and also modern fiction. The series has five grades: the *Introductory Grade* at a 1400 word level, *Grade 1* at a 2100 word level, *Grade 2* at a 3100 word level, *Grade 3* at a 3700 word level and *Grade 4* which consists of abridged stories. Structural as well as lexical controls are applied at each level.

Wherever possible the mood and style of the original stories have been retained. Where this requires departure from the grading scheme, definitions and notes are given.

All the books in the series are attractively illustrated. Each book also has a short section containing questions and suggested activities for students.

Stories of Shakespeare's Plays 1

Retold by N. Kates

Hong Kong
OXFORD UNIVERSITY PRESS
Oxford Singapore Tokyo

Oxford University Press

Oxford New York Toronto
Petaling Jaya Singapore Hong Kong Tokyo
Delhi Bombay Calcutta Madras Karachi
Nairobi Dar es Salaam Cape Town
Melbourne Auckland

and associated companies in
Beirut Berlin Ibadan Nicosia

This adaptation first published 1972
Fourteenth impression 1986

Retold by N. Kates
Illustrated by Priscilla Keung
Cover artwork by Kathryn Blomfield
Simplified according to the language grading scheme
especially compiled by D.H. Howe

ISBN 0 19 638227 0

Printed in Hong Kong by Nordica Printing Co.
Published by Oxford University Press, Warwick House, Hong Kong

Contents

A Midsummer Night's Dream

Introduction

This is a story about some people who lived in Athens, a city in Greece, a long time ago. At that time, the girls in Athens did not choose their own husbands, as most of them do today. The father of the family told his daughter whom she was to marry. There was also a law which said that if she refused to obey him, her father could have his daughter put to death. When Hermia's father will not let her marry Lysander, the two young people decide to run away. Meeting in the woods at night, they are seen by the elves and fairies who are small, playful but unreal people who use their magic to help man or make trouble for him.

Chapter 1

Prince Theseus was going to be married. His future wife was Hippolyta, Queen of the Amazons. He was planning many parties for her. One day, just before his wedding, an old man named Egeus came to ask for the Prince's advice. Egeus had chosen a man named Demetrius as husband for his daughter, Hermia. She said she would not marry Demetrius because she loved another young man, called Lysander. Her father said she must do as he told her, or die.

The Prince told Hermia that she must obey her father, but she still refused. She said that her best friend, Helena, loved Demetrius, and that he ought to marry her. Theseus felt sorry for Hermia. Because he was the Prince, he could not oppose* the law. He told her that she must either marry Demetrius, or spend the rest of her life in a religious house away from her home and friends. The Prince was to be married in four days' time. Hermia was allowed those four days in which to give her answer.

Hermia was very unhappy and went to see Lysander. Together they planned to run away. Lysander had a rich aunt who lived twenty miles from Athens. The Athenian laws could not touch them there.

'We can go to her house,' said Lysander, 'and be married there. Tomorrow night, creep secretly from your father's house. Meet me in the wood where we used to play when we were children.'

While they were talking, Helena joined them. As she was Hermia's best friend, they told her what they were going to do. Helena, instead of keeping their secret, told Demetrius all about it. She hoped that Demetrius would follow Hermia to the wood. She would go and look for him there.

**oppose*, to go against.

Chapter 2

The wood, where Hermia and Lysander had played when they were young, was the home of elves and fairies.* These little people played games all night in the open spaces of the wood. Recently their fun had been spoiled. Oberon and Titania, their King and Queen, were angry with each other. When they quarrelled, the elves and fairies ran and hid because they were afraid. The cause of their quarrel was a little boy. The Queen had stolen him from his home, and had made him her servant-boy. Oberon wanted the boy for himself, but Titania would not leave him.

On the night when Hermia and Lysander were to meet in the wood, Titania and Oberon had also met and were quarrelling about the boy. Oberon again asked Titania to give him the boy, but she refused. When they parted Oberon was very angry. He planned a way of making her do as he wanted. He called to one of his little elves called Puck. Puck was a naughty little elf. He liked to play tricks on the village people. He turned their milk bad. He stole their cream. He knocked over an old woman's chair as she was about to sit on it, and so on. He was Oberon's messenger-boy.

'Come here, Puck,' said Oberon. 'Bring me the flower which is called "love-in-idleness". It is a magic flower. When its juice is put onto the eyes of people who are asleep, they fall in love with the first thing they see when they wake up. I will put some of the juice of the flower onto the eyes of Titania when she is asleep. When she opens her eyes, she will fall in love with the first thing she looks at, whatever it may be. And before I take away the

**elves and fairies*, small, unreal people who can do magic.

magic, I will make her give me that child to be *my* servant-boy.'

Puck went off to find the flower. This was just the kind of work he enjoyed. While Oberon was waiting for him to return, Demetrius looking for Hermia, and Helena following Demetrius, entered the wood. Oberon, who could make himself invisible,* watched them and listened to them talking. He heard Demetrius scold Helena for following him.

'I don't love you, so please stop following me. Go away!' he said.

Helena said that even if he did not love her, she still loved him. She would continue to follow him, whether he allowed her to do so or not. Demetrius was angry and ran off into the bushes. He hoped she could not follow him there, but she still went after him.

Oberon watched her disappear into the bushy wood. He felt very sorry for her, and decided to help her. He would use the love-juice, which Puck was bringing him, to make Demetrius fall in love with Helena. So when Puck returned with the juice, he said to him, 'In this wood there is a sweet Athenian lady. She is in love with a young man who keeps running away from her. Go and find them. Put the juice on his eyes, and do it in such a way that the next thing he sees will be the lady. You will know the man by his Athenian dress.'

Puck went away to do this new work. Oberon, who had kept some of the juice, went to look for Titania. Still invisible, he watched her giving her fairies their orders for the night. Some were to bring a special kind of bird's wings to make fairy coats. Others were to kill the bad insects in the flowers. Some were to keep away the night bird whose cry might keep Titania awake, and

**invisible,* cannot be seen.

some of them had to stay by her, to sing her softly to sleep.

As soon as she slept, Oberon pressed some of the juice on her eyes. As he did so he said, 'The first thing you see when you wake up you will fall in love with.' Then he left her.

Chapter 3

Now, Hermia and Lysander had also met in the wood. They were on their way to Lysander's aunt's house, but lost the path. Hermia was tired and so they sat down for a rest. It was not long before they both fell asleep.

Puck was running through the wood to do as Oberon had told him. He found Hermia and Lysander still asleep. Because Lysander was wearing Athenian clothes, and Hermia was an Athenian girl, he thought that these were the two people he had been sent to find. So he quickly pressed the love-juice on Lysander's eyes and went away.

Everything would have been all right if the first person Lysander looked at when he awoke had been Hermia. He loved her already. But during the night, Helena came by. In the dark she could not see Hermia and Lysander, and as she was tired she also lay down to sleep. She lay quite close to Lysander, without knowing it. And when he awoke, Helena was the first person he saw. So of course he fell very much in love with her.

However, when Lysander spoke lovingly to Helena, she thought he was making fun of her. She knew that he was in love with Hermia. She was hurt and angry, and ran away from him. But he went after her, forgetting all about Hermia.

Hermia woke up. She had been dreaming, and her dream had frightened her. She wanted to tell Lysander about it, but he was nowhere to be seen. She walked on and on in the wood, calling Lysander's name.

So now the four young people were separated in different parts of the wood — Helena looking for Demetrius, Lysander looking for Helena, and Hermia looking for Lysander.

Chapter 4

In the early hours of the morning, some more people entered the wood. They were workmen from the village. One of them had written a play. They had come to the wood to practise their parts. Their acting was really very bad, but they took it very seriously.

Puck had finished the work which Oberon had given him to do, and he was on his way back to find the King. He saw these workmen acting. In the middle of their acting, he played one of his tricks upon them. On the head of the most foolish and funny of them, Bottom the Weaver, he dropped a covering with a shape like the head of a donkey. Frightened by this magical happening, the rest of the actors ran away.

Titania was asleep near by, and it was this ugly creature that she first saw when she woke up. Because of the love-juice, she fell in love with him! She madc Bottom sing for her. She made a circle of flowers and put it on his head. She sang him to sleep with lovely songs. While she was doing all this, Oberon came and scolded her for behaving so foolishly. Titania felt so silly that she readily gave him the stolen child which had been the cause of all their quarrelling.

Now that he had got what he wanted, Oberon took away the magic which had made Titania fall in love with Bottom. He told Puck to take away the donkey's head which he had put on Bottom, and they all left him. The man went to look for his friends, asking himself what had happened to him.

Chapter 5

Hermia was still looking for her lost Lysander. On her way through the wood, she met Demetrius. Oberon was close by, and he heard them talking. He heard Hermia tell Demetrius that she thought he had done something bad to Lysander. She asked him to bring Lysander back to her. Demetrius did not understand her, and left her to continue looking alone.

Oberon wanted to set things right between the lovers.* He sent Puck to find Helena and bring her to where Demetrius was sleeping. He himself dropped the juice on Demetrius's eyes. He hoped that when Demetrius awoke he would see Helena and love her. Then Lysander and Hermia, Helena and Demetrius would be happy together.

But this happy end was not to be. For Helena and Lysander came together to where Demetrius was asleep. When he woke, Demetrius first looked at Helena and fell in love with her. He too began to speak lovingly to her. Helena, who before had not been loved by either of the two men, was very surprised. She thought that they had joined together to make fun of her.

Then Hermia came towards them. She had once been loved by both Lysander and Demetrius, but now she was not loved by either! She asked Lysander why he had left her. But he only answered her rudely and Demetrius turned away from her. Helena thought this all so strange that she was sure that all three had planned together to to make fun of her. Hermia accused Helena of having stolen her lover, and while these two were quarrelling, Lysander and Demetrius went away to fight with swords. The winner would marry Helena.

**lover*, a person who is in love, or is loved.

At last Oberon thought of a way to make things end happily for the lovers. He commanded Puck to stop Lysander and Demetrius meeting and fighting. By copying their voices, he was to make them want to fight. But he was to hide them from each other in a thick cloud, so that they could not meet and hurt each other.

'Do this until they are tired,' said Oberon. 'When they fall asleep, drop the juice of this other flower into Lysander's eye. This will make him remember his love for Hermia again. Demetrius will still be in love with Helena.'

Puck did as he was told. Then he led the lovers about in the wood so that in the end they all went to sleep near the same spot.

Chapter 6

Hermia was the first to wake. When she found her lost Lysander asleep near her, she began to ask herself why he had left her so strangely and why he had come back. Did he still love her? Lysander, when he woke, became his usual self once more. He loved Hermia as much as ever. For Helena too, the night ended happily. She awoke to find that Demetrius really did love her. Hermia and Helena became friends again.

However, they could still not be truly happy. Old Egeus had said that his daughter Hermia was to marry Demetrius, or die. What could they do about that cruel law?

They did not have to worry for long. Prince Theseus and Queen Hippolyta were out hunting* in the early hours of the morning. With them had come Hermia's father, Egeus. As they were riding through the wood, they met the young lovers. Of course Theseus wanted to know what they were doing in the wood so early. Lysander told him how Hermia and he had planned to meet there and run away from Athens and the cruel law.

When Egeus heard this, he at once said that they would be punished for trying to cheat Demetrius.

But Demetrius, feeling rather foolish, then explained that he no longer wanted Hermia. He was now in love with Helena. When Prince Theseus found the four of them so happy he made Egeus agree not to punish them. He also arranged that the happy pairs should be married on his wedding day.

So the unlucky happenings of a midsummer night had a happy ending after all.

**hunt,* to go after animals for food or sport.

Twelfth Night

Introduction

There once lived in the land of Greece a brother and a sister, called Sebastian and Viola. They were twins* and looked very much alike. If they were dressed in the same sort of clothes, their friends found it difficult to know who was the boy and who was the girl. Their father had died when they were thirteen years old. They loved each other very much, and were never really happy except when they were together.

When this story begins, Sebastian and his sister are on a ship going to Illyria. There is a bad storm and the ship is broken into pieces by the sea. Many people are drowned, but Viola is lucky. With the captain and a few sailors, she is able to get to the shore in a small boat.

**twins,* two children born at the same time to the same mother.

Chapter 1

When she had stepped out of the boat, Viola asked the captain if he knew where they were.

'This is Illyria, lady,' said the captain.

Viola was very sad because Sebastian was not with her. She hoped that he had been lucky too, and that he was still alive. The captain told her that he had seen Sebastian tie himself to a strong piece of wood before the ship sank. There was a good chance that he had been saved also. This was good news, and Viola began to feel happier. She looked around her and asked herself what she ought to do. The captain told her that he knew the country well. He had been born there. The land was ruled over by a Prince named Orsino. He was a good man, but just now he was unhappy. He loved a lady named Olivia, and wanted to marry her, but she did not love him.

'Who is Olivia?' asked Viola. The captain told her that Olivia was the daughter of a rich man who had died a year ago. After his death, Olivia was looked after by her brother. But he too had died, and Olivia was so sad that she never left the house or let anyone go to visit her. Viola felt very sorry for the poor lady. She knew how it felt to lose a much loved brother. She wanted to go and work for Olivia as her servant, but the captain said that she could not. Since her brother died, Olivia had allowed no one to enter the house, not even Prince Orsino, who loved her.

'Then,' said Viola, 'if I cannot work for the lady, I shall work for the Prince himself. You, captain, must help me, and I will pay you well. Get me some clothes and I will dress myself as a young man. Then take me to the Prince and tell him I want to be his servant-boy. I will sing to him and work hard for him. But do not tell anyone who I really am.' The captain agreed to Viola's plan and he promised to keep her secret.

Viola gave him some money and he bought her the clothes she wanted. When she was dressed in the clothes, she looked exactly like her brother, Sebastian. Then the captain took Viola to see the Prince. Orsino liked the look of the boy (he thought Viola was a boy) and agreed that he should be his servant. Viola now called herself Cesario, and no one but the captain knew that she was a girl dressed as a boy.

Viola worked hard and Orsino was very pleased with her. He told her all about his love for Olivia. The lady refused to see him. She would not keep the presents and letters he sent to her by his messengers. Viola, as she listened to his story, began to fall in love with him. But she did not show her love for her master.

One day, the Prince sent Viola with a love-letter to Olivia. 'Go to the lady,' he said, 'and tell her that I love her. Although she is unkind I love nobody but her. You are still a boy and she may listen to you. She would send an older man away without letting him in.'

So, although Viola herself loved the Prince, she went to Olivia's house to try to make the lady marry him. She felt very unhappy as she walked along. When she arrived at the door of Olivia's house, the servant would not let her in.

'The lady is ill,' he said, 'and no one may see her.'

'I know she is ill,' replied Viola, 'that is why I have come. I will not go away until you let me in.'

'But she is asleep,' said the man. 'No one can see her now.'

'That too I know,' said Viola, 'but still I will not go until I have talked to her.'

The servant went away and told Olivia about Viola.

He said that the young 'man' would not go until he had talked to her. Olivia asked what he was like. When she heard that he was young and good-looking she was eager to see him, and told her servant to let the visitor in. She felt sure that the messenger had come from Orsino. She covered her face with a veil,* saying that once more she would hear what the Prince had to say to her.

**veil,* covering of fine net or other cloth to protect or hide a woman's face.

Chapter 2

The servant took Viola into a room where several ladies were sitting. One of the ladies had a veil over her face. Viola did not know which lady was Olivia. She said that she had learnt the words she was to say so carefully that it would be silly to say them to the wrong person. At last, after a lot of talking, she learnt that the lady with the veil was Olivia. But she still refused to give her the message until everyone else had left the room.

'My words are for your ears alone,' she said, 'and I ask you to let me see your face as I speak to you.'

Now Olivia liked the look of the young man, and the way he spoke. She was far more interested in the messenger himself than in any message he might have brought her from the Prince. So she was quite willing for him to see her face.

When the other ladies had left the room, she took off her veil. As she did so she said, 'I will pull the curtain, and show you the picture. Do you think it is well painted?'

'Very well,' replied the servant-boy, 'you are very beautiful.'

Then Viola told Olivia about Prince Orsino's love; how he thought about her night and day; and how sad he was because she did not love him.

'I shall never love your master,' said Olivia. 'Go back and tell him so. I want no more messages from him. But *you* may come again to tell me how he acts when he hears my message.' The fact was that Olivia was quickly falling in love with Viola whom she believed was a man. She could not bear to think she might never see him again. Then she offered him some money, but Viola refused to take it. Viola asked her once again to think kindly of the Prince, then she went away.

When the 'young man' had gone, Olivia was surprised to find how quickly she had fallen in love with him. She tried to think of a way in which she could show Cesario that she loved him, and so make him come back to her. After thinking for a minute or two, she took off her ring and gave it to her servant, Malvolio.

'Run after the Prince's messenger,' she said to him, 'and give him this ring which he left behind. Tell him I will not accept it, nor any other presents from his master. Tell him also that, if he comes again tomorrow, I will explain why I am acting in this way.'

Malvolio did as he was asked. When she saw the ring, Viola knew that Orsino had not sent it with her. She guessed that Olivia was falling in love with her and wanted to see her again. This was, of course, just what Olivia had hoped.

'Poor lady,' thought Viola, 'it's no use her falling in love with me. Even though I am dressed as a man, I'm still a woman. I love the Prince. The Prince loves Olivia. Olivia loves me. It is a problem too difficult for me to work out. I can only hope that, in time, everything will end happily.'

Chapter 3

When Viola got back to the Prince's palace,* she told Orsino that her visit had done no good. The lady had said she could never love him. But the Prince would not believe that Olivia meant what she said. Viola tried to tell him that it was useless to keep on hoping.

'If a lady loved you,' she said, 'and you did not love her, you would tell her so. And she would have to take "No" for an answer.'

'That may be so,' answered the Prince, 'but women can't love in the same way as men. No lady could love me as much as I love Olivia!'

'I know they can,' replied Viola. Then she told him how her father's daughter once loved a man, and never told him so, but suffered* in secret. Orsino never guessed that she was speaking of herself, and of her love for him. He thought she was telling him about her sister.

Orsino told her to go again to Olivia and ask her to marry him. He gave her a jewel to take as a present for the lady. Viola left once more for Olivia's house.

This time the servant let her in at once, and she was shown into Olivia's room. She began again to ask Olivia to be kind to Orsino, but Olivia refused to listen to her.

'But if you have anything to say about yourself,' Olivia said, 'then I will listen gladly.'

Viola did not seem to understand her, so Olivia told her that she was in love with her. Viola did not know what to do or say. So she left the house, and told Olivia that she could never love a woman.

**palace,* the house of a King or Prince.
**suffered,* was very unhappy or felt pain.

Chapter 4

All this time, Viola had never given up hope of seeing her lost brother again. That day, while she was talking to Olivia, a sea-captain and a young man entered the town. The captain's name was Antonio, and the young man was Sebastian, Viola's twin-brother. He had not been drowned. After tying himself to a piece of wood and floating for a time on the sea, he had been picked up by Antonio's ship, alive and unhurt. The captain of the ship had been kind to him, and they were soon good friends. Three months later they reached Illyria. They landed near the place where Viola had first stepped onto the shore.

Sebastian wanted to see the town and visit the Prince's palace. Antonio thought it might not be safe for Sebastian to go alone, but he was frightened to go with him. In a recent sea-fight, he had hurt the Prince's nephew, and the Prince had given orders for him to be made prisoner. If he went into the town, someone might know who he was. So he went a little way with Sebastian and then told him to go on alone. He gave Sebastian his purse because he might need some money in the town, and he told him to keep out of danger.

* * * * *

At this time, also, other things were happening, which must now be described.

Olivia had an uncle called Sir Toby Belch, who was very fat. He drank too often and too much. For a long time he had been trying to take his friend, Sir Andrew Aguecheek, to meet Olivia. This made her angry. She did not like the man. He was wild and boastful, but a terrible coward.

One day Olivia's servant, Malvolio, made Sir Toby angry by scolding him for drinking too much. Now Malvolio was a very proud man. He thought that he was a wonderful person. Everybody hated him because he thought too much of himself. Olivia's girl-servant, Maria, helped Sir Toby to play a trick on Malvolio, to make him look stupid. She wrote a letter, copying Olivia's writing, and signing Olivia's name. The letter was addressed to Malvolio. In it Maria made it seem as if Olivia was in love with her servant, and was writing secretly to him. Malvolio found the letter and fell right into the trap. When he went to see Olivia he made a great fool of himself.

Sir Toby Belch was pleased at this joke and wanted another. So he decided to play a trick on Sir Andrew Aguecheek and Viola. Sir Andrew had seen Viola when she visited Olivia, and was very jealous because the boy seemed to be Olivia's favourite. Sir Toby told him that he ought to have knocked Cesario down, and that Olivia thought he was stupid for not doing so. He said that Sir Andrew must fight Cesario (Viola) and show Olivia what a brave man he was. So Sir Andrew asked Viola to fight with him. Viola was frightened. Sir Toby told her that Sir Andrew Aguecheek was a terrible man to fight with. Then he told his friend the same story about Viola, so that he frightened Sir Andrew almost as much as he had frightened the poor girl. The two agreed to fight, believing what Sir Toby told them, though they were afraid of each other.

Chapter 5

Sir Andrew Aguecheek and Viola met in the garden of Olivia's house. The fight was about to begin when a stranger arrived. He pulled out his sword and said that he would fight instead of Viola. The stranger was Antonio. He had come to town to look for Sebastian. When he saw Viola in men's clothes, he thought that she was Sebastian. Viola was very surprised, but very pleased that he had come to help her.

Of course, Antonio had taken a great risk in coming into the town. Almost at once he was seen by some of the Prince's officers, who happened to be passing by, and they made him their prisoner. Before they took him away, Antonio turned to Viola (whom he still thought was Sebastian) and said, 'I must obey. See what has happened because I came into the town to look for you. Please give me back my purse, I shall need it.'

Viola was very puzzled. Here was a man, whom she had never seen before, asking for a purse which she had not got. She offered the captain half the money she had with her, which was not very much, to pay for the help he had given her.

Antonio was very hurt. His young friend refused to give him back his purse, and was pretending not to know who he was! He told the officers that he had saved this young man's life, looked after him and made him his friend. The officers were not interested in the story. They wanted him to go with them at once. So Antonio, still scolding Viola for her behaviour and calling her Sebastian, was led away. Viola guessed that the captain had mistaken her for her brother. She would have liked to talk to Antonio, but he had gone. So she left the place afraid that, if she stayed, she might have to fight again.

Soon Sebastian, who was walking round the town, came to Olivia's garden. Sir Andrew saw him and thought he was Cesario. Sir Andrew was feeling very brave now, and he rushed at Sebastian and struck him on the head. Sebastian was not a coward. He returned the blow and pulled out his sword, telling Sir Andrew to do the same. They had not been fighting for long when Olivia came out of her house. When she saw her dear Cesario (as she thought) in danger, she called out for them to stop. She ordered Sir Andrew to go away, and took Sebastian into her house.

Now Sebastian was very surprised at the kindness shown to him by a lady he had never seen before. He was even more surprised at the loving words she used when speaking to him. He asked himself if he was asleep or dreaming. If he *was* dreaming, he liked the dream and hoped it would continue! He thought the lady might be mad, although she did not seem to be. But he could not explain this love which she showed to him.

After a while, Olivia sent for the priest* and asked Sebastian to marry her. Sebastian, although he was very surprised, agreed, for he liked her very much. Olivia promised him that the marriage would stay a secret for as long as he wished. They were married by the priest, and then Sebastian left his new wife. He wanted to find Antonio and ask his friend's advice about these strange happenings.

**priest,* a holy man.

Chapter 6

Viola returned to her master. She told him that Olivia did not want to hear his name ever again. Orsino decided it was time that he went to see Olivia himself. So, taking Viola and some servants with him, he started out for Olivia's house. When they arrived at the door, they met one of Olivia's servants. Orsino promised him some money if he could manage to get Olivia to come out of her house. The man hurried off to do so, and the Prince, his servants and Viola waited outside.

As they stood there, the officers of the law, who had caught Antonio, came along the street with their prisoner. They were looking for the Prince. When they saw Orsino they led Antonio up to him and told him that this was the man who had hurt his nephew. They had found him fighting in the street and had caught him. When Viola heard what they said, she told her master how Antonio had helped her, although he was a stranger to her.

Now Antonio still thought that Viola was his friend, Sebastian. So, when he heard her words, he explained angrily to the Prince how he had dragged this boy, half-drowned, from the sea. He told what had happened since that morning when they landed on the shore; how he had followed the boy, afraid that he might get into trouble, even though he knew he might be caught; how the boy was now acting very badly in return for all his kindness, by refusing to give back his purse and pretending not to know who he was.

'You are speaking like a madman,' said the Prince. 'For the last three months this boy has been with me, working in my palace. But here comes Olivia. Officers, take him away, I will speak to him later.'

Then, turning to Olivia, he said how cruelly she had acted towards him. But Olivia would not listen to him. Instead, she spoke lovingly to Cesario and smiled sweetly at him. Orsino began to see what had happened. The servant-boy whom he had sent so often to Olivia had made her fall in love with him. He spoke angrily to Cesario and turned to go. He ordered Cesario to follow him. Viola was only too happy to obey. She had been feeling very uncomfortable because Olivia was showing her so much attention. So, though Olivia asked her several times to stay, she followed her master. As she went, she said to Olivia that she loved her master more than her own life, and more than she would ever love a wife.

Then Olivia forgot her promise to keep her marriage a secret. She cried out, 'Cesario, my husband, stay!'

'Husband?' repeated the Prince in great surprise.

'Yes, my husband,' replied Olivia, 'he will tell you so.'

'No, my lord, I am not her husband,' said Viola.

Olivia sent for the priest who had married her to Sebastian. The priest said he had certainly married these two, only two hours ago. Though Viola cried again and again that it was not true, that she was not married to Olivia, the Prince did not believe her. He told her he never wanted to see her again, and turned to go. Everyone was puzzled by what had happened. Olivia was hurt and surprised by Viola saying that they were not married. Viola could not understand why the priest should say that she had been to a wedding when she knew she had not been there at all.

Then Sebastian arrived. He first spoke friendly words of greeting to Olivia, calling her his wife. Next he turned eagerly to Antonio, and told him how pleased he was to see him. Everyone looked surprised when they saw

Viola and Sebastian so much alike in looks and voice, standing in front of them. No one could tell which was Cesario. But the surprise of the brother and sister was greatest of all.

'If you were a woman,' said Sebastian, 'I would think that you were my sister, Viola, whom I believe drowned. But I have no brother.'

Viola was now able to tell everyone that she was not really a man, but was Sebastian's sister. She told them how she had bought the clothes she was wearing so that she could go and work for the Prince.

Now that the puzzle was explained, Sebastian turned to Olivia and laughed at her for falling in love with a woman, and having married a man by mistake. But Olivia seemed happy with the way things had ended. Orsino, seeing that Olivia was really married to another man, remembered how often Cesario had said he would never love a woman as much as he loved his master. He asked Viola to marry him and made her say again that she loved him. Then he took her away, promising that as soon as she was dressed again in a woman's clothes, she would no longer be his servant-boy, but his wife.

Romeo and Juliet

Introduction

In the city of Verona, in Italy, there lived two very rich families. One was named Montague, the other Capulet. These two families had been quarrelling with each other for a long time. The quarrel was so bad that if members of the Capulet family met Montagues in the street they fought each other. They never went into each other's houses.

In this story Romeo, the son of Montague, falls in love with Juliet, the daughter of Capulet. Their love for each other is beautiful and true but ends in sadness and death because of the quarrel between their two families.

Chapter 1

Romeo, son of Lord Montague, thought he was in love with a beautiful lady called Rosaline. She, however, cared nothing for him. He was very unhappy. He followed her everywhere, trying to make her love him.

At the time this story begins, old Lord Capulet plans to hold a party. He has asked many beautiful young ladies, including Rosaline, and many good-looking young men. But he has not asked anyone from the Montague family.

Romeo and his cousin, Benvolio, were out walking in the streets of Verona. Capulet's servant, who was delivering letters inviting people to his master's party, spoke to them. He could not read, and he asked Romeo, not knowing who Romeo was, to read the names on the letters for him. When Romeo saw that Rosaline was going to the party, he decided that he would go too. Benvolio agreed to go with him, and they took Mercutio, a close relative of the Prince of Verona, as well. So that no one would know who they were, they all wore masks.*

When the three friends, their faces carefully covered, arrived at the party, they were greeted by old Lord Capulet. He did not know that behind the masks were members of the enemy family. He told them to enjoy themselves. So they joined freely in the music and dancing.

And then a strange thing happened to Romeo. Till now he had looked at no other lady but Rosaline. Suddenly, among the people dancing, he saw a lady even

**mask,* covering for the face to prevent people from seeing who one is.

more beautiful than Rosaline. He felt he must meet her and speak to her.

Unluckily for Romeo, a nephew of Capulet, Tybalt, had seen who he was. Tybalt was very angry with Romeo for coming to the party without being invited. He wanted a chance to kill Romeo. But his uncle, the old Lord Capulet, told him not to be so angry. Lord Capulet spoke well of Romeo and refused to let him be hurt while he was a guest in his house. Tybalt, however, wanted to hurt Romeo and waited for a better chance.

Chapter 2

Romeo did not know that Tybalt had seen who he was. As soon as he could, he went up to the beautiful lady that he had just seen, and spoke to her. He told her that he had fallen in love with her, and she spoke very kindly to him. But as they were talking, the lady was called away to see her mother. Romeo was left asking himself who she was. He turned to the nurse who had called her, and learned that he had been talking to the daughter of Lord Capulet himself! He was sorry to find that she was the daughter of his enemy, but he knew he would happily risk his life to win her love.

Juliet, too, was worried when she heard from her nurse the name of the young man to whom she had been speaking. She was now in love with her father's enemy.

The guests went away at midnight. Romeo left his friends as they were on their way home, and went back to the house. He jumped over the wall of the fruit-garden which went all the way round the house. Here he stood for some time, thinking of his new love. Suddenly Juliet appeared at the open window above him. At first she did not see her lover, but spoke his name sadly several times. She cried because he belonged to the hated family of Montague.

Romeo, listening from below, knew from her words that she was in love with him. He called softly to her, and they talked for a long time about the love they felt for each other. At last, Juliet's nurse called to her. It was time she went to rest. Juliet promised Romeo that she would send a messenger to him next day. Romeo must tell the messenger where Juliet was to meet her lover for their wedding. And so they said good-night and Romeo left the garden.

Romeo, however, did not go to his own house. He went to ask the advice of his good friend, Friar* Lawrence. The friar was up early that morning, and was in his garden picking flowers when Romeo came to him. From the look on Romeo's face, and the early hour of the visit, the friar guessed that something was wrong. When Romeo told him how he had spent the night, and of his love for Juliet, the friar was, at first, not pleased. But he could see how serious Romeo was; and he hoped that perhaps a marriage between the Capulets and Montagues might help them to become friends once more.

So he agreed to do as Romeo asked, and promised to conduct the marriage between him and Juliet. They arranged that the marriage would take place that afternoon. When Juliet's messenger arrived, Romeo said that Juliet must meet him at Friar Lawrence's house.

After the wedding, Juliet returned to her home and waited for Romeo to come and see her. He had told her that he would come secretly to the garden round her house, and would take her away with him. Unluckily, something happened which stopped the newly married pair from meeting again that day.

**friar*, a holy man.

Chapter 3

At about the same time that Romeo and Juliet were being married, Benvolio and Mercutio were walking in the streets of Verona. Suddenly, they saw a group of Capulets coming towards them. Leading the group was Tybalt. He was the man who had seen Romeo at the party given by old Lord Capulet.

Now Mercutio did not belong to either of the enemy families, but as he was a friend of Romeo, a Montague, Tybalt came up to him and accused him of that friendship. There was a quarrel, and Tybalt was just about to start fighting with Mercutio, when Romeo himself came that way. Tybalt turned his attention to Romeo and called him a wicked man. Romeo of course did not want to quarrel with Tybalt, who was a cousin of his dear Juliet. So he spoke to him in a friendly way. Mercutio was angry with Romeo for speaking to Tybalt like this, and took out his sword to fight Tybalt himself.

In the fight which followed, Benvolio and Romeo did their best to stop the spilling of blood. But Tybalt struck a blow which hurt Mercutio badly. Then, seeing Mercutio lying on the ground, Tybalt and his friends ran away.

Romeo could see that Mercutio had not long to live. Benvolio helped the dying man into a house near by, and the doctor was sent for. While this was happening, Tybalt had returned to try and find Romeo. Romeo was so unhappy, seeing Mercutio so cruelly killed, that he fought with Tybalt and killed him.

Benvolio came back and found Romeo standing beside the dead body of Tybalt. He told Romeo to go quickly, before anyone in the watching crowd thought of making him a prisoner.

However, someone had already gone to the Prince of Verona, to tell him what had happened. The Prince had forbidden fighting in the streets, and was soon on his way to where the fight had taken place. He took with him Lord Montague, Lord Capulet and their wives. He demanded to know why there had been a fight. Benvolio explained how Romeo had not meant to fight Tybalt. But because Tybalt had killed Mercutio, Romeo had become angry and had taken Tybalt's life.

Lady Capulet wanted Romeo put to death for what he had done. Lord Montague said that Romeo had done the right thing in killing a murderer.* The Prince, who wanted no trouble, ordered Romeo to leave the country. He did not want murder in the streets of Verona to go unpunished.

Juliet was still waiting for her Romeo to come to take her away. Her nurse brought her the terrible news that Romeo had killed her cousin, Tybalt. At first Juliet was angry at what he had done, for she did not know how hard he had tried to stop the fight. But, when she heard that Romeo had been sent out of the country, her love for him became stronger than her anger. She was glad that Tybalt, who would have killed Romeo, had been killed first. Yet she was very sad that she would be separated from her husband.

Juliet's nurse, who had brought the sad news, now spoke comfortingly to her. She knew where Romeo was hiding, and thought that perhaps he could at least come and say good-bye to his wife, before he left.

**murderer,* someone who kills a person.

Chapter 4

When Romeo ran away from the fight, he went to see Friar Lawrence. He told the old man everything that had happened. He was expecting to be put to death. When he found out later that the Prince had ordered him to leave the country, this seemed just as terrible a punishment. He hated the idea of being separated from his Juliet.

At last, a message came from Juliet asking Romeo to see her. This made him a little happier. He would now at least have a chance to say good-bye before he went away. Friar Lawrence tried to make him cheerful. He hoped that there might be a happy end to all this trouble. Both Romeo and Juliet were alive and well, and perhaps the Prince might forgive Romeo. Their marriage might still bring to an end the quarrel between the two families. The priest advised Romeo to stay for a while in Mantua, which was not far away. There he would hear all the news from Verona, and must wait for the right time to return and ask the Prince to forgive him. To this advice Romeo now listened, and got ready to go and see Juliet before he left the country.

Both joyful and sad was this second meeting at night, when the rest of the family were in bed. Romeo and Juliet were happy to be together again, even if it was only for a few hours. At the same time, they were sad because they had to part, perhaps for ever. As the sun began to rise, Romeo decided it was time for him to go. If the people of the house, who were now awaking, discovered him, they would take his life.

Romeo promised to write to Juliet from Mantua. He told her that they might one day be able to live happily together. He kissed her good-bye, and softly went away.

Chapter 5

In the early morning, Juliet's mother, Lady Capulet, came into her daughter's room. She found Juliet pale and tearful. She thought that Juliet was crying because of the death of her cousin, Tybalt. Lady Capulet had now brought news that she hoped would make Juliet forget what had happened. She hoped this news would be a happy surprise for her daughter.

Old Lord Capulet, not knowing about Juliet's marriage to Romeo, had chosen a husband for her. The man's name was Count Paris, and he was rich and good-looking. Lord Capulet thought that Juliet would be pleased and proud to have Paris as her husband. There was no reason for delay, and the marriage had been arranged to take place in a few days' time.

This was the news which her mother told Juliet. But instead of making Juliet happy, this news, as you may imagine, only made her sad. She thought of many excuses to try to stop the arranged marriage. She said she did not know Paris well enough to marry him; that she was still too young to get married; it was too soon after the death of her cousin, Tybalt. She could not tell her parents the real reason why she could not marry Paris; that she was married already.

Her parents were angry. Her father thought she was being difficult for no good reason, and ordered her, speaking very cruelly, to be ready to marry Paris on the next Thursday. Then he walked out of the room.

Juliet turned to her mother, hoping that she would help her to delay the marriage, but Lady Capulet followed her husband out. Even her old nurse, whom Juliet had told about her marriage, was against her. She said that since Juliet could not have Romeo, it was foolish of her to refuse to marry Paris.

Poor Juliet! She at last decided to go to see Friar Lawrence to ask his advice. She told her parents she was going to talk to him about the wedding. The friar already knew of the coming marriage. Count Paris had visited him to arrange things for it, and was still there when Juliet arrived. Paris left, as it would not be proper for him to stay while Juliet was with the friar.

'I shall come for you,' he said to her, 'early on Thursday morning.'

Alone with the friar, Juliet asked for his help and advice. She would do anything, rather than give up Romeo and have to marry Paris. She would even kill herself if necessary. The good friar, who loved both Romeo and Juliet, told her how he thought they might be able to stop the wedding. His plan would need a lot of bravery.

'Go home,' he said, 'and be happy. Say you will marry Paris. Tomorrow is Wednesday; sleep alone tomorrow night. Don't let your nurse stay in the room with you. Take this bottle, and when you are in bed, drink the liquid* in it.' Friar Lawrence put a small bottle into her hand. He said that when Juliet had drunk what was inside it, she would lie as if dead, for forty-two hours afterwards. So that when Paris came to get her in the morning, he would certainly think she was dead.

She would then be taken to the family tomb.* If, therefore, she was brave enough to let all this happen to her, she would wake, as if from a dream, in forty-two hours. 'I shall send a message to Romeo,' said the friar, 'I shall ask him to come to the tomb to meet you when you

*liquid, something which can be poured, like water.

*tomb, a place where dead bodies are put, a small room, often under the ground.

wake, and take you away with him to Mantua.'

Juliet was pleased with the plan, She went home, ready to do as Friar Lawrence had directed. She found her parents busy arranging the marriage party. As she now seemed ready to obey her father's wishes, he was very pleased that she had been to see the friar.

'I am sorry,' said Juliet. 'I will marry Paris, if that is what you want.' She pretended to be interested in choosing her wedding dress and the jewels she would wear. She asked her nurse to leave her alone that night, telling her to go and help Lady Capulet instead.

When the time came, it needed all her bravery to drink the dangerous liquid. Could it be poison* that the friar had given her? But no, he was too good and kind to do that. Or what if she woke too soon in the dark room under the ground, amongst the bones of the dead? The idea made her very frightened. Then she remembered Romeo, and how much she loved him. She drank the liquid; and at once became lifeless.

At the same time, happy because Juliet had decided to marry Paris, her family got ready for the next day's wedding. Her father was up very early next morning. He heard Paris and his people coming, and asked the nurse to call Juliet.

'Go and wake Juliet, and dress her properly! I will go and talk to Paris. Hurry up! Hurry up! The future husband has already arrived. Hurry up, I say!'

But when the nurse entered Juliet's room she could not believe her eyes. At first she thought that the girl was sleeping, and tried to wake her. It was no use. Juliet did not move, but lay there, her cheeks pale, her arms and legs stiff and cold.

Very frightened, the nurse called to the parents. They

**poison,* a drink, or food, which may kill.

all thought Juliet was dead. Everyone in the house was puzzled, frightened and disappointed. Paris could not speak, he was so surprised. Friar Lawrence was the only person in the house who stayed calm. He tried to comfort Juliet's parents, and asked them to get things ready for the funeral. And so the day which had begun so happily for the family ended sadly. The body of Juliet was carried away to be buried.

Chapter 6

The news of Juliet's funeral quickly reached Romeo at Mantua. But he had not yet received the message from Friar Lawrence, telling him that Juliet was not really dead, but was waiting for him to go to her. So of course, when his servant told him the sad news, Romeo was terribly unhappy. He thought he would go and have a last look at Juliet, even though she was dead. He asked his servant to get him a horse for the journey. Then he went to a shop near by to buy some poison. He had decided that, as Juliet was dead, he would die also. He did not want to go on living without her.

Romeo arrived in Verona in the middle of the night. He went to the church where he knew the Capulets had their family tomb. He lit a lamp that he had brought with him, and began to break open the room in which the dead Capulets lay. As he was doing this, he heard someone say, 'O wicked Montague!' It was the young Count Paris, who had come to see the tomb of the girl who should have been his wife. He did not know of Romeo's love for Juliet. He knew how the Capulets and Montagues hated each other, and thought that Romeo had come to do something terrible to the dead bodies of his enemies. So he angrily asked Romeo to stop.

Romeo told Paris he would kill him if he did not go away. They started to fight, and Paris was killed. As he died, he cried, 'If you are a kind man, open this tomb and lay me with Juliet.' Romeo picked up his lamp to see who it was that he had killed. He saw Paris whom, he had heard, was going to marry Juliet. He felt sorry for him, so he lifted the body and laid it beside Juliet in the tomb. Then he took a last look at his Juliet, gave her a last kiss, quietly drank his poison, and died.

It was nearly time for Juliet to wake up. Friar Lawrence came alone to the tomb with a spade* and an iron bar. The messenger whom he had sent to Mantua, had not arrived there. There had been an accident on the way. When the friar heard about it he hurried to the tomb, so that he would be there when Juliet woke up. He did not think that Romeo would be there. But as he walked in the dark towards the church, Romeo's servant came towards him. He had stayed away from the tomb, as Romeo had ordered him not to go near. This man showed the friar where the tomb was. The friar felt his way along, feeling very much afraid. What was that light he could see burning just outside the tomb? What were those spots of blood on the ground? Whose bodies were these? He came near and saw Romeo and Paris lying dead beside Juliet. And Juliet was just beginning to wake from her long sleep.

Juliet opened her eyes and saw the friar standing beside her. Slowly, she began to remember where she was. 'Where is my Romeo?' she asked the friar.

Friar Lawrence was just going to reply, when he heard voices. People were coming to the tomb. The servant of Paris had run away when he saw his master fighting with Romeo, and was now bringing the night watchmen* back with him. The friar was afraid of being found with the dead bodies, and asked Juliet to come away quickly and hide. But Juliet had seen Romeo by her side, and would not move. So the priest went by himself, and hid a little way off.

Then Juliet saw that Romeo was dead, with the poison-cup still in his hand. She at once knew that he must have drunk the poison because he thought that she

**spade*, a tool for digging.

**watchmen*, men paid to guard the church.

was dead. Taking Romeo's knife from his belt, Juliet pushed it into her own heart.

When the night watchmen saw the three dead bodies and the signs of a fight, they would not let the servants of Paris and Romeo go away. They also kept the old friar, who had been found hiding near by. They sent for the Prince of Verona and the parents of Romeo, Juliet and Paris.

And there, outside the tomb, the sad old friar told them the whole story. Here are his words:

'Romeo there, dead, was Juliet's husband and she, there, dead, was Romeo's wife.' He pointed to them as he spoke. 'I married them. Their wedding-day was the day on which Tybalt was killed and Romeo was sent away. Juliet was unhappy because Romeo had to leave her, not because of the death of her cousin, Tybalt. And you,' the friar pointed to Lord Capulet, 'told her she must marry Count Paris. She came to me and asked me to find some way to save her from this second marriage. I gave her a sleeping medicine to take so that she would look dead. I wrote to Romeo, asking him to be here tonight to help me to take Juliet away. But my messenger was stopped by an accident, and last evening my letter was returned to me. So I came alone to take Juliet from the tomb, when she awoke. I was going to keep her with me in secret until I could send for Romeo. When I got here, I found Paris and Romeo dead. Then Juliet awoke. She asked for Romeo, and I was about to tell her what had happened, when I heard voices. I asked her to come and hide, but she had seen Romeo and would not leave him. Then she must have killed herself.'

The servant of Paris told how the fight had started, and Romeo's servant described how his master had ridden that night from Mantua. So the whole sad story became clear.

At last the Prince of Verona, turning to Lord Montague and Lord Capulet, told them that if they had ended the quarrelling between their two families long ago, this terrible thing might not have happened. And so at last the two old men turned to one another and promised each other friendship and peace.

As You Like It

Introduction

Long ago, in the land of France, there lived a Prince. He had no palace or lands of his own. They had all been taken from him by his wicked younger brother. He now lived in the Forest of Arden, a beautiful wood in a corner of the country which he had once ruled as his own. Some of his good friends and servants had gone with him. They would rather live there, in the open air, than work for the wicked younger brother in his palace. But though the Prince had many good friends with him in the forest, his daughter, Rosalind, was not there. She had wanted to go with her father, but the younger Prince, Frederick, had kept her at his palace to be a friend to his own daughter, Celia. The two girls liked each other very much. Rosalind was often sad when she thought about her father, and Celia did all she could to help her cousin to be happy.

Chapter 1

Rosalind and Celia were sitting in the palace garden. A messenger came to tell Celia that her father wanted her. Frederick had arranged a wrestling* match. In his palace he had a man who was a famous wrestler. The man's name was Charles. He was so strong that he had never lost a match. He was *very* clever, and he had just thrown three brothers, one after the other, and had nearly killed them. Celia and Rosalind felt frightened at the idea of going to see something as cruel as a wrestling match. The Prince arrived, and told them that the match would take place in the garden where they were sitting, so they would have to stay and see it. Prince Frederick told them that a very young man, who had come to fight Charles, would probably get hurt. He had asked the man not to fight, but he said he wanted to. He asked the two girls to speak to the young man. Perhaps they could make him decide not to fight.

Rosalind and Celia talked to the young man and asked him not to wrestle.

'It does not matter if I die,' he said, 'for I have no friends. I shall fight, and you must wish me luck!'

Rosalind and Celia did so, and Rosalind said, 'I wish that the little strength which I have might be added to yours.' He left the two girls, and the wrestling match began.

Now this good-looking young stranger was called Orlando. His father had been a friend of the Prince in the Forest of Arden. His father had died when Orlando was a small boy, and Orlando had lived with his brother Oliver ever since. Oliver was a wicked man. He had

**wrestling,* a struggle between two men in which each one tries to throw the other to the ground.

always been very unkind to his young brother. He did not send him to school. He did not let him have lessons at home. However, Orlando had grown into a good, kind young man, like his dead father. Oliver hated him because he had made many friends and was liked by everybody he met.

When Orlando decided to fight with the wrestler, Oliver soon heard about it. Charles the Wrestler himself went to tell Oliver. He was afraid that if he hurt Orlando, Oliver would be angry with him. But Oliver thought he now had a good chance of really hurting his brother. So he said to the wrestler, 'My brother is not a good man. He is always trying to hurt me, his own brother. He does not listen to me. I advised him not to fight with you, but he took no notice. Therefore let him be punished. I want you to break his neck. If you only hurt him a little, you may be sure he will come back to you and kill you for it. There is no one I know who is more wicked than he is.' When the wrestler heard this, he went away, promising that he would show no kindness to Orlando.

Oliver then went to Orlando and wished him luck in the fight. It was because of his unhappy life at home that Orlando had said that it did not matter if he lost, or was killed in the fight.

But Rosalind didn't want him to be killed. As the fight began, she prayed that he would win. Perhaps her prayers helped Orlando. He showed that he was a better wrestler than Charles. He threw Charles heavily, and the wrestler lay on the ground, unable to move or speak.

The match was over, and Orlando had won. The Prince asked Orlando who he was. When, however, Orlando told him his father's name, the Prince was not pleased. For Orlando's father had been a close friend of his elder brother.

'I wish you had been the son of any other man,' he said, and left the garden. He was angry that the son of his old enemy had been successful in the fight.

Rosalind was very happy when she heard what Orlando's name was. She had fallen in love with the brave young man. She was glad that he was the son of her father's friend. Going up to him, she took a gold chain from around her neck, and gave it to him.

'Wear this for me,' she said, 'I would give you more if I could.'

Orlando, who had received very little kindness in his life, was very pleased. He thought how lovely Rosalind was, and fell in love with her. But, before they could talk together any more, someone told Orlando that Prince Frederick was now his enemy. It would not be safe for him to stay there. So he left the palace at once.

Chapter 2

Rosalind and Celia returned to the palace. Rosalind felt sad because Orlando had gone away. Celia tried to make her cheerful, but it was no use.

Prince Frederick was not pleased with Rosalind. She was good and kind, and the people felt sorry for her because her father had been sent away. Perhaps, also, he was angry with her for liking Orlando, whom he hated.

While Celia and Rosalind were talking about Orlando, the Prince himself entered the room. He ordered Rosalind to leave the palace at once. 'If, in ten days' time, you are found any nearer to this palace than twenty miles, you will die,' he said.

Poor Rosalind asked what she had done to make him so angry with her. 'You are your father's daughter; that is enough!' was the only answer he gave her.

Celia spoke to her father, and asked him to let Rosalind stay, but it was no good. The Prince would say no more. He repeated his command, and left the room.

But Celia liked her cousin too much to let her go alone. 'In sending you away,' she said, 'my father has also sent me away. I don't care what you say, I am coming with you.'

So they decided that they would go together. They would try to find Rosalind's father in the Forest of Arden. But to travel through the country in their rich-looking dresses would be dangerous.

'Let us put on plain and poor clothes,' said Celia, 'and paint our faces, so that people will think that we are country people.'

'And we shall be safer, too, if one of us is dressed as a man,' said Rosalind. 'I should be the one to do that, because I am taller.'

* * * * *

As well as changing their dress, the two girls changed their names. From now on Rosalind was to be called Ganymede, and Celia called herself Aliena. When they had dressed themselves, they collected their money and jewels, and left the palace without being seen.

At the same time as Rosalind and Celia were planning to escape from Prince Frederick, Orlando was also planning to escape from his cruel brother. He had returned home after the wrestling match, and had been met at the gate by a servant. The man's name was Adam, and he had always loved Orlando and served him well.

'My dear master,' said Adam, 'you must not stay here. Your brother, Oliver, has heard how you won the wrestling match. He is so angry at your success that he means to set fire to the room you will sleep in tonight. If that plan fails, then I'm sure he will find another way of killing you. Keep away from his house.'

'But Adam,' said Orlando, 'where am I to go? I have no money and I cannot go about stealing food.'

The old servant replied that he had enough money to give Orlando. He would go with him, for he did not want to stay with the wicked Oliver.

'O good old man!' cried Orlando. 'We will go together. And I hope that before all your money has been spent, we shall find some way of earning a living.'

So Adam and his master set out together. Their journey took them towards the Forest of Arden, where the good Prince, Rosalind's father, and his friends had their camp.

Chapter 3

Rosalind and Celia, dressed like country people, reached the edge of the Forest of Arden in safety. In this part of the country there were no inns* where they could buy food and find shelter. They walked here and there through the trees, till they were tired and hungry. Rosalind felt very near to crying, but she remembered that she was no longer Rosalind, a woman, but Ganymede, a man. She could not burst into tears. At last they met two shepherds* and asked them where they could buy food and where they could stay for the night.

'This young girl,' said Rosalind, 'is so hungry and tired that she cannot walk any more. Please tell us where we can find food and shelter for the night. We have plenty of money to pay for it.'

One of the shepherds replied, 'There is little I can do for you. The sheep which you see are not my own. My master is selling them, and the house in which I live.'

'Then we shall buy the house, the sheep and the grass-land from him,' said Rosalind. 'We will pay you too, if you will stay on and look after the sheep for us.'

So the shepherd, whose name was Corin, gave them food and shelter and they bought the house and stayed there. After resting for some time, they decided that they would try to discover where in the forest the Prince lived.

All this time, Rosalind never forgot Orlando. She knew that she loved him, and wanted to see him again. She did not know that he, too, had left home. She did not know that he, with his old servant, Adam, had gone in the same

**inn,* an old name for a hotel.
**shepherds,* men who look after sheep.

direction as she and Celia, and was also in the Forest of Arden.

* * * * *

When Orlando and Adam reached the forest, they found that it was difficult to get food and shelter. For a long time they walked round and round under the trees. But the old man, ill from hunger, soon asked to be left to die where he was. Orlando carried him to the shelter of a big tree, and laid him down comfortably. 'Don't talk of dying, Adam,' he said. 'Rest here while I go and get something for us to eat. I shall come back very soon.'

Now the good Prince and his friends had made their camp close to this place. They were sitting under some trees and the Prince had just begun to eat a meal. Orlando, looking for food, saw them. Because he needed food so badly, he ran up to them. He pulled out his sword and cried, 'Eat no more, eat no more, give me food!'

The Prince was very surprised at first, but when Orlando had explained everything, he told the young man to go and bring old Adam. He promised that they could have some food when they got back to the camp.

When Orlando returned with Adam, the Prince kept his word. They were given as much food as they could eat. When the Prince discovered that Orlando was the son of his old friend, he was very pleased. He told them that they could stay at his camp for as long as they wanted.

Chapter 4

The house where Rosalind and Celia were living was not far away from the Prince's camp. One day, before they had been there long, Rosalind had a strange surprise. She found her name written on some trees. There were poems written about her, too. She could not think who had done it. She asked Celia about it, but she did not know either. It was even more strange because Rosalind was still dressed as a man. The writing must have been done by someone who had known her before she came to this place.

As they were talking about it, they saw two men coming towards them. The girls hid themselves and, as the men came nearer, Rosalind saw that one of them was Orlando. His friend was making fun of him for writing poems to Rosalind on the trees. The young ladies came out of their hiding-place, and spoke to Orlando. He did not know them and thought that Rosalind was a shepherd-boy. They became good friends, and she, dressed as Ganymede, talked with him about his love for Rosalind. She offered to help him to find a cure for his love.

So the days passed happily. Rosalind even forgot that she was looking for her father, the Prince. Then one day he met her in the forest. He noticed how this shepherd-boy looked very much like his own daughter. He stopped her and asked her what her name was, and who her parents were. She replied that her name was Ganymede and that her parents were as good as his. The Prince was very amused. He never thought that she was speaking the truth.

* * * * *

Soon after this meeting of Rosalind with her father,

a strange adventure happened to Orlando. He was walking alone in the forest when he saw someone lying asleep under a tree. He was surprised when he saw who the stranger was. It was Oliver, his cruel brother. He was dressed in torn, old clothes. His face was dirty and he looked most unhappy. As he looked closer, Orlando saw that a snake had wound itself around his brother's neck. When it saw Orlando, the snake slid away into the bushes. Orlando watched it go, and saw a terrible animal hiding in the bushes, waiting to jump out at the sleeping man.

For a moment, Orlando thought that he would let the animal kill Oliver. Why should he help Oliver who had always been so cruel to him? But Orlando was too kind to let his brother die, and too brave to run away from the animal. He ran quickly forward and attacked it with his sword. He killed it, but not before it had hurt his arm. The noise of the fight woke Oliver. At first he could not believe what he saw. There stood the brother whom he hated, but who had just saved his life. He felt very sorry for his past behaviour, and asked Orlando to forgive him. Orlando did forgive him, and from that day Oliver loved Orlando as a brother should.

Oliver had come to the forest to kill his brother. He had been sent to look for him by Prince Frederick. After the wrestling match, the Prince had decided to have Orlando killed. But Orlando had gone away before he could be taken prisoner. Oliver had been ordered to bring Orlando back, dead or alive. If he could not do so by the end of a year, he would lose all his money and lands. So Oliver had gone to look for his brother, but had got lost in the forest, and had gone to sleep. Then Orlando had come along. and the rest of the story has been told.

Chapter 5

At midday on the day when Orlando saved his brother's life, he had promised to meet his friend, Ganymede. But, because of his adventure with the wild animal, he could not keep his promise. So, to show why he could not come, he sent Oliver with a handkerchief covered with blood from his arm.

Rosalind, still dressed as a man, was waiting for Orlando when Oliver came up to her. He explained who he was, and gave her the handkerchief. When she heard that it was her lover's blood which was on the cloth, Rosalind almost fainted,* but she remembered, just in time, that she was dressed as a man. She tried to explain that she had only pretended to faint, and sent Oliver back to Orlando.

But now Rosalind and Orlando were not the only people in love. For Oliver had met Celia and had fallen in love with her, and she with him. So Oliver had a lot to tell Orlando when he returned.

'When I showed him your handkerchief,' he said, 'your friend, Ganymede, almost fainted.' Then he told him how Celia and he had fallen in love and were going to be married. 'As for our father's lands,' he added, 'I give them all to you.'

Orlando was very happy for his brother. 'Let your wedding be tomorrow,' he said, 'I will ask the Prince and his friends to come to it.' Oliver went to find Celia to tell her the good news.

Rosalind came to see Orlando. Ever since she had heard that her lover had been hurt by a wild animal, she had wanted to come and see him. She was pleased to see that he was not badly hurt. Orlando told her that Celia and Oliver were getting married the next day.

**fainted (v. to faint),* fell down as if dead.

'I am very glad,' he said, 'for my brother will marry the girl he loves. But oh, if only I could marry my dear Rosalind!'

When Rosalind heard him say this she thought that it was time for her to change back to herself once more. 'If you wish to marry Rosalind tomorrow,' she said, 'tomorrow Rosalind shall appear, and you shall have your wish. Believe me, I can make your Rosalind appear, for since I was three years old, I have lived with a man of magic. With his help, I shall be able to do as I have promised.'

Orlando almost believed what she said. 'Put on your best clothes and invite your friends,' Rosalind continued. 'If your wish is to marry Rosalind tomorrow, then you shall.'

On the next day, therefore, all of them met. Ganymede went with Orlando to the Prince.

'If I bring in your daughter, Rosalind,' Ganymede said to the Prince, 'will you let her marry Orlando?'

'I will,' the Prince replied.

'And do you say that you will marry Rosalind, Orlando, if I bring her here?'

'I will marry her,' said Orlando.

Ganymede and Aliena then left, as if to get ready for the wedding. Ganymede took off her man's clothing, and put on a woman's dress, like Rosalind's. And Aliena changed her poor country dress for one of her own, and appeared as Celia once more.

Then they went back to the Prince and Orlando. Rosalind went straight to her father and kissed him. Orlando, looking at her, saw that she was Rosalind, whom he had wanted so much to see again.

The Prince told Rosalind that he was very happy that she was to marry Orlando. He greeted Celia, his niece,

and Oliver. So they were married in the forest, and afterwards they had a party.

While they were all still eating and drinking, a messenger arrived, with news for the Prince. 'Your wicked brother,' he said, 'has given you back your country.'

He told them all how Prince Frederick had got an army and had started out meaning to attack his brother in the Forest of Arden. But as he had entered the forest, he had met a man of God. This man had talked with him for a long time and, at last, Frederick saw how wicked he had been. He decided to give up everything, and to spend the rest of his life in a religious house. So he sent a message to his brother, promising to give him back his country. He also promised the Prince's friends that they could have back their money and lands.

So the story ended happily for the Prince and the lovers.

Questions

A Midsummer Night's Dream

Chapter 1
1. What was the name of the man whom Hermia wanted to marry?
2. Why did Egeus forbid his daughter to marry the man of her choice?
3. Can you give other words which mean the same as 'religious house'?
4. Why did Helena tell Demetrius that Hermia and Lysander were going to run away together?

Chapter 2
1. Oberon and Titania quarrelled. What was it all about?
2. What did the flower 'love-in-idleness' do to people?
3. Who found the flower for Oberon?
4. Oberon could do many magic things. In the story we hear of one of them. What was it?
5. What were the things which the fairies had to do for Titania?

Chapter 3
1. Puck made a bad mistake. What was it?
2. What made Helena think that Lysander was making fun of her?
3. Say what happened to Hermia when she woke up.

Chapter 4
1. What did Puck do while he was on his way back to Oberon?
2. Why did Titania give Oberon the little boy?

Chapter 5
1. Demetrius and Lysander arranged to fight. Why?
2. How did Puck stop the two men from hurting each other during the fight?
3. What did Oberon tell Puck to do when the fight was over?

Chapter 6
1. What might the Prince and the Queen have been hunting in the wood?
2. Did Egeus make his daughter marry Demetrius?
3. When did the happy pairs get married?

Twelfth Night

Chapter 1
1. Why did the captain think that Sebastian was still alive?
2. For whom did Viola feel sorry, and why?
3. What made Viola decide to dress up as a man?
4. What did Viola call herself when she was dressed as a man?
5. Orsino wanted Viola to ask Olivia to marry him. How do you imagine she could do this?
6. What did Olivia do to her face before Viola entered the room?

Chapter 2
1. Olivia said, 'I will pull the curtain and show you the picture.' What did she mean?
2. What happened to Olivia when she saw Cesario?
3. What did Olivia ask her servant, Malvolio, to do for her?

Chapter 3
1. The Prince did not believe that Olivia would never love him. How did Viola try to show him that it was useless to go on hoping?
2. When Viola went back to Olivia, did Olivia listen to her message?
3. What made Viola say that she 'could never love a woman'?

Chapter 4
1. How had Sebastian's life been saved?
2. Why didn't Antonio go into town with his friend?
3. How did Maria play a trick on Malvolio?
4. What did Sir Toby tell Sir Andrew he must do to Viola?
5. How did Sir Toby frighten Viola and Sir Andrew?

Chapter 5
1. Why did Antonio say he would fight instead of Viola?
2. What did he ask Viola to do for him before he was taken away?
3. Was Viola able to do what he asked?
4. How did Sebastian manage to marry Olivia?

Chapter 6
1. Why did the Prince disbelieve Antonio's story?
2. How did Olivia give away her secret?
3. Why was everybody surprised when they saw Sebastian?

Romeo And Juliet

Chapter 1

1. Why didn't the Capulets and Montagues speak to each other?
2. To which family did Romeo belong?
3. How did Romeo find out that Rosaline was going to Lord Capulet's party?
4. How did Romeo and his friends get into Lord Capulet's house without anyone seeing who they were?
5. Who knew Romeo at the party?
6. Was Lord Capulet angry with Romeo for coming to his party?

Chapter 2

1. Romeo fell in love with a lady at the party. Who was she?
2. What did Romeo do when he left the Capulets' house?
3. Juliet was to send a messenger to Romeo next morning. What was the message he would take?
4. Whom did Romeo ask for advice?
5. What did Friar Lawrence hope might happen if Romeo and Juliet were married?

Chapter 3

1. Who was Mercutio?
2. Why did he fight Tybalt?
3. What brought the Prince to the place where Romeo had killed Tybalt?
4. What piece of news did the nurse bring Juliet? How did she comfort her mistress?

Chapter 4

1. How did Romeo feel when he heard that he must leave the country?
2. What advice did Friar Lawrence give to Romeo?

Chapter 5

1. Lady Capulet had some good news for her daughter. What was it, and how did Juliet feel about it?
2. Where did Juliet go for help?
3. What was Friar Lawrence able to do for Juliet?
4. What happened next morning?

Chapter 6

1. What did Romeo do when he heard that Juliet was dead?
2. Why did Romeo kill Paris?

3. What brought Friar Lawrence to the tomb?
4. What did Juliet do when she woke up?
5. Why did the Capulets and Montagues decide to be friends?

As You Like It

Chapter 1
1. Why was Charles the Wrestler so famous?
2. Why was Orlando willing to risk his life in the wrestling match?
3. What lies did Oliver tell Charles about his brother, Orlando?
4. What made Prince Frederick angry with Orlando, after he had won the fight?

Chapter 2
1. Why did Prince Frederick tell Rosalind that she had to leave his palace?
2. How did the two girls decide they would dress for their journey?
3. What made Orlando decide to leave home?

Chapter 3
1. How did Rosalind and Celia find food and shelter?
2. What happened to Orlando when he went to look for food?

Chapter 4
1. What strange things did Rosalind see on the trees in the wood?
2. How did she find out that Orlando loved her?
3. What did Rosalind say to the Prince when she met him, and he asked who her parents were?
4. Orlando found his brother, Oliver, in the wood. Describe what happened at their meeting.
5. Why had Oliver come to look for Orlando?

Chapter 5
1. How did Rosalind nearly give herself away when Oliver came to speak to her?
2. How did Rosalind explain to Orlando that she would make his lover appear?
3. What had happened to Prince Frederick?

Oxford Progressive English Readers

Introductory Grade

Vocabulary restricted to 1400 headwords
Illustrated in full colour

The Call of the Wild and Other Stories	Jack London
Emma	Jane Austen
Jungle Book Stories	Rudyard Kipling
Life Without Katy and Seven Other Stories	O. Henry
Little Women	Louisa M. Alcott
The Lost Umbrella of Kim Chu	Eleanor Estes
Stories from Vanity Fair	W.M. Thackeray
Tales from the Arabian Nights	Retold by Rosemary Border
Treasure Island	R.L. Stevenson

Grade 1

Vocabulary restricted to 2100 headwords
Illustrated in full colour

The Adventures of Sherlock Holmes	Sir Arthur Conan Doyle
Alice's Adventures in Wonderland	Lewis Carroll
A Christmas Carol	Charles Dickens
The Dagger and Wings and Other Father Brown Stories	G.K. Chesterton
The Flying Heads and Other Strange Stories	Retold by C. Nancarrow
The Golden Touch and Other Stories	Retold by R. Border
Great Expectations	Charles Dickens
Gulliver's Travels	Jonathan Swift
Hijacked!	J.M. Marks
Jane Eyre	Charlotte Brontë
Lord Jim	Joseph Conrad
Oliver Twist	Charles Dickens
The Stone Junk	Retold by D.H. Howe
Stories of Shakespeare's Plays 1	Retold by N. Kates
Tales from Tolstoy	Retold by R.D. Binfield
The Talking Tree and Other Stories	David McRobbie
The Treasure of the Sierra Madre	B. Traven
True Grit	Charles Portis

Grade 2

Vocabulary restricted to 3100 headwords
Illustrated in colour

The Adventures of Tom Sawyer	Mark Twain
Alice's Adventures through the Looking Glass	Lewis Carroll
Around the World in Eighty Days	Jules Verne
Border Kidnap	J.M. Marks
David Copperfield	Charles Dickens
Five Tales	Oscar Wilde
Fog and Other Stories	Bill Lowe
Further Adventures of Sherlock Holmes	Sir Arthur Conan Doyle